MOZART
AND
THE MASONS

1   Wolfgang Amadeus Mozart,
silhouette by J. H. Löschenkohl,
1785; from the *Musik- und
Theater-Almanach auf das Jahr
1786*.

MOZART
AND
THE MASONS

NEW LIGHT ON THE LODGE
"CROWNED HOPE"

H. C. ROBBINS LANDON

THAMES AND HUDSON

This is the fourteenth of the annual Walter Neurath Memorial Lectures on subjects reflecting the interests of the founder of Thames and Hudson. The Directors wish to express particular gratitude to the Governors and Master of Birkbeck College, University of London, for their gracious sponsorship of these lectures.

*First published in the USA in 1983 by Thames and Hudson Inc.,
500 Fifth Avenue, New York, New York 10110*

First paperback edition, with new preface and minor corrections, 1991

Library of Congress Catalog card number 82–60140

Printed and bound in Singapore by C. S. Graphics

PREFACE TO THE SECOND EDITION

This book began life as the fourteenth in the series of Walter Neurath Memorial Lectures. The subject of this lecture had been my recent research on Mozart and the Freemasons' lodges with which he was associated in Vienna. The discovery of an ms. membership list of the Lodge 'Zur gekrönten Hoffnung' ('Crowned Hope') with detailed indications of those present and absent in 1790, as well as the names of the presiding officers and dignitaries, made it possible to identify positively a well-known oil painting in the Historisches Museum der Stadt Wien as depicting a meeting of the Lodge 'Crowned Hope' in 1790, an occasion on which Mozart himself was present and is prominently portrayed.

Subsequently, I discovered another membership list, this one in printed form, in the library of Melk Abbey in Lower Austria; it was reproduced in my book *Mozart: the Golden Years, 1781–1791* (Thames and Hudson, 1989), which also included new information concerning members of Mozart's second Lodge – the first had been 'Zur Wohlthätigkeit' ('Beneficence') from 1784 to 1786 – especially with regard to members of the Esterházy family.

Documentary evidence of a previously unknown lawsuit involving Prince Carl Lichnowsky, who had been a fellow member of Mozart's lodge in 1784–6, has been recently discovered in the Hofkammerarchiv in Vienna. It reveals that on 12 November 1791 Mozart was ordered to repay a debt of 1,435 florins and 32 kreuzer, together with 24 florins costs, by having half his salary as Imperial Royal Chamber Composer deducted and by sequestration of his goods and chattels. Curiously, this sum does not appear in the list of debts prepared after the composer's death on 5 December 1791 (the so-called Suspense Order). No explanation for this extraordinary court case is known, but it must have been a contributory factor in hastening the composer's early death.

Concerning the authorship of the 'Little Masonic Cantata' (K.623) mentioned on p. 56, it now appears that the new lodge was an offshoot of Emanuel Schikaneder's lodge in Regensburg, of which he was still listed as a member in 1791. This matter is being investigated by a Viennese colleague, Walter Brauneis.

Château de Foncoussières
March 1991   H.C.R.L.

On 5 December 1784, the Viennese Freemasons' Lodge 'Zur Wohlthätigkeit' ('Beneficence') circulated the following document[1] to its sister Lodges:

> Proposed Kapellmeister Mozart. – Our former Sec'y Bro. Hoffman forgot to register this proposed member at the most honourable sister ☐ ☐. He was already proposed four weeks ago at the honourable district ☐ and we should like therefore in the coming week to take steps for his admission if the most honourable sister ☐ ☐ have no objections to him.
>
> In the Orient of Vienna
>
> 57 $\overline{\text{XII}}^{\,5}$ 84   Schwanckhardt: Secr:

On 14 December Mozart was duly initiated in the Lodge 'Zur Wohlthätigkeit' as an Entered Apprentice, and thus became a member of the Craft.

In England Freemasonry in an organized form began to spread its influence following the founding of the Grand Lodge in London on 24 June 1717, the Feast of St John the Baptist, and it was under the flag of St John that the European Lodges were founded. In Austria the first Lodge was founded on 17 September 1742 by members of the Lodge 'Three Skeletons' in Breslau; the new Austrian Lodge was called 'Aux Trois Canons'. Freemasonry flourished in the Austrian Crown Lands and in neighbouring Bohemia and Hungary, not least because of the example set by Francis Stephen, Duke of Lorraine and husband of the Archduchess (later Empress) Maria Theresa: he had become a member of the Craft in May 1731. A Papal Bull of 1738,[2] which condemned Freemasonry, was simply suppressed in Austria, since Maria Theresa regarded such Papal action as an infringement of her privileges. The

Empress did not approve of Freemasonry, however, and her son Joseph II, who co-reigned with his mother from 1765 (following the death of his father, Francis Stephen) to 1780, regarded the Craft with considerable, if tolerant, scepticism.

Most of the Austrian Lodges adhered to the English ritual and the ancient Landmarks, but on 26 March 1781 – by which time Joseph II reigned alone – an Imperial Decree prescribed that no spiritual or secular orders were to submit to a foreign authority, nor were such orders permitted to pay money or fees to any body outside the Monarchy. Thus, on 22 April 1784, the 'Große Landesloge von Österreich' (the Grand Lodge of Austria) was constituted. This new Grand Lodge embraced seven Provinces: Austria – seventeen Lodges; Bohemia – seven Lodges; Lemberg (Galicia) – four Lodges; Austrian Lombardy – two Lodges; Transylvania – three Lodges; Hungary – twelve Lodges; Austrian Netherlands – seventeen Lodges.

During the first half of the 1780s, Freemasonry flourished in Vienna. The Craft drew to its ranks leading figures from all walks of life. The membership lists, many of which by some miracle – since the Craft was forbidden in Austria from 1795 to 1918 – have survived, include the names of counts and princes, senior military officers, writers, musicians, bankers and merchants. Of the eight St John Lodges in Vienna the leading one was 'Zur wahren Eintracht' ('True Concord'), founded in 1781 and having by 1785, when Mozart began to visit it frequently, some 200 members under the Master, Ignaz von Born, a distinguished scientist, writer and mineralogist, whom Mozart and Schikaneder are purported to have used as the model for Sarastro in *Die Zauberflöte*.

Mozart's small Lodge 'Zur Wohlthätigkeit' was founded on 2 February 1783, and its members found it expedient to work within the larger, more influential Lodge 'Zur wahren Eintracht', in which case the 'Wohlthätigkeit' Brothers would sign the attendance register as visitors. The Master of Mozart's Lodge was the writer Otto, *Freiherr* (Baron) von Gemmingen-Hornberg, Palatine Chamberlain and Privy Councillor, who had been Mozart's protector at Mannheim in 1778 and in 1782 moved to Vienna; it was he, presumably, who first suggested to the young composer that he join the Craft.

2 Ignaz von Born, Master of the Lodge 'Zur
wahren Eintracht'; silhouette by Gonord, 1781.

3 The seal of the Viennese Lodge 'Zur
Wohlthätigkeit', 1783; from the *Journal für
Freimaurer*, 1784.

Apart from the large and influential Lodge 'Zur wahren Eintracht'
and the equally large 'Zur gekrönten Hoffnung' ('Crowned Hope'), as
well as Mozart's 'Zur Wohlthätigkeit', there were in 1785 five other,
small Lodges in Vienna. The first two (in alphabetical order) were 'Zu
den drei Adlern' ('Three Eagles') and 'Zur Bestandigkeit' ('Steadfastness'), to the second of which belonged *inter alia* Ludwig Karl Fischer,
the first Osmin in Mozart's *Die Entführung aus dem Serail*, and the
composer's brother-in-law, Joseph Lange (who would, towards the
end of Mozart's life, paint the greatest extant, albeit unfinished, portrait

9

of the composer); another member of 'Steadfastness' was Christoph Torricella, publisher of works by Haydn and Mozart. The other smaller Viennese Lodges were: 'Zu den drei Feuern' ('Three Fires'; founded in 1783); 'Zum heiligen Joseph' ('Saint Joseph'), to which belonged Lorenz Leopold Haschka, later noted as author of the Emperor's Hymn, set to music by Haydn in 1797; and 'Zum Palmbaum' ('Palm Tree'). It was into this thriving Masonic community that Mozart entered at the end of 1784. We find him on Christmas Eve in attendance at 'Zur wahren Eintracht' and, on 7 January 1785, he was passed to the Fellow-Craft Degree under the Master, Ignaz von Born. There is no surviving record of when Mozart was raised to the Third Degree, that of Master Mason.

The year 1784 is significant in Mozart's life not only for his first connections with the Masons, but also because in February of that year he began to keep a thematic catalogue of his works which provides many precise dates which would otherwise be unknown to us; he continued to make entries in the catalogue until a fortnight before he died.[3] This catalogue is also vital for its valuable information about the Masonic works therein recorded.

On 29 December 1784, a fortnight after Mozart joined the Craft, his friend Joseph Haydn, Princely Esterházy *Capellmeister*, applied to the Master of Ceremonies at the Lodge 'Zur wahren Eintracht', Franz Philipp von Weber, asking him to intercede on Haydn's behalf with a view to his joining the Masons. On 24 January 1785, Haydn was proposed and accepted, and 28 January was set as the date for his initiation. Mozart came to welcome his friend, but Haydn was not there. The news of the date proposed for his initiation had reached Eszterháza Castle too late for him to travel to Vienna, and a new date had to be established: 11 February. Haydn duly arrived and was initiated as an Entered Apprentice, but this time Mozart could not attend the ceremony; on that same Friday, his father Leopold had arrived from Salzburg, and that evening Wolfgang gave the first of his six subscription concerts at the 'Mehlgrube' on the Neuer Markt, playing the solo part in the first performance of his piano Concerto in D minor, K.466.

4 The only known entrance ticket for a concert given by Mozart in Vienna; now in the collection of the Mozarteum, Salzburg.

5, 6 The title on the cover of Mozart's autograph catalogue of his works composed from February 1784 until shortly before his death in 1791, and (*overleaf*) two pages listing works composed in 1784: four piano Concertos (K.449, 450, 451 and 453) and, second from bottom, the Quintet for piano, oboe, clarinet, horn and bassoon (K.452).

1784.

Den 9ten Hornung.

†/ † Ein Klavierkonzert. begleitung. 2 violini, viola e Basso. (2 oboe, 2 corni ad li...

Den 15ten März.

2, Ein Klavier Konzert. begleitung. 2 violini e 2 viole, 1 flauto, 2 oboe, 2 fagotti,
2 corni e Basso.

Den 22ten.

†3,† Ein Klavierkonzert. begleitung. 2 violini, 2 viole, 1 flauto, 2 oboe, 2 fagotti,
† 2 corni, 2 clarini, timpany e Basso.

Den 30ten.

4, Ein Klavier Quintett. begleitung. 1 oboe, 1 clarinetto, 1 corno, et 1 fagotto.

Den 12ten April.

5† Ein Klavier Konzert. begleitung. 2 violini, 2 viole, 1 flauto, 2 oboe, 2 fagotti,
† 2 corni, e Basso.

On the next day, Saturday, 12 February, there was a string quartet party at Mozart's beautiful apartment in the Domgasse, in the shadow of the great Gothic Cathedral of St Stephen's. We learn of the events from a letter from Leopold Mozart to his daughter, Maria Anna (Nannerl), in St Gilgen; the evening was to celebrate Haydn's initiation, and two of his Lodge's Brethren, the Barons Tinti, were also present. Leopold Mozart writes:[4]

> Saturday Evening Herr Joseph Haydn and the two Barons Tindi [*sic*] were here; the new Quartets were played, the three new ones that he [Wolfgang] wrote to go with the other three which we already own; they are a little easier than the others, but brilliantly composed. Herr Haydn said to me: 'I tell you before God, and as an honest man, that your son is the greatest composer I know, either personally or by reputation. He has taste and, apart from that, the greatest knowledge of composition.'

Opposite

7 A page from the Finale of Mozart's piano Concerto in D minor (K.466), showing the composer's exploitation of the upper and lower ranges of the piano.

8 Joseph Haydn, anonymous miniature painted on ivory, *c.* 1785.

9 The Mozart family, oil painting by J. N. della Croce, *c.* 1780 1. The composer and his sister Nannerl are at the keyboard, with their father Leopold holding his violin; behind them is a portrait of Mozart's mother (who had died in 1778).

Al mio caro Amico Haydn

Un Padre, avendo risolto di mandare i suoi figlj nel gran
Mondo, stimò doverli affidare alla protezione, e condotta
d'un Uomo molto celebre in allora, il quale per buona sorte,
era di più il suo migliore Amico. — Eccoti dunque del pari,
Uom celebre, ed Amico mio carisimo i sei miei figlj. — Essi sono,
è vero il frutto di una lunga, e laboriosa fatica, pur la speranza
fattami da più Amici di vederla almeno in parte compensata,
m'incoraggisce, e mi lusinga, che questi parti siano per essermi
un giorno di qualche consolazione. — Tu stesso Amico carisimo,
nell'ultimo tuo Soggiorno in questa Capitale, me ne dimostrasti
la tua soddisfazione. — Questo tuo suffragio mi anima sopra
tutto, perchè Io te li raccommandi, e mi fa sperare, che non ti
sembreranno del tutto indegni del tuo favore. — Piacciati dunque
accoglierli benignamente, ed esser loro Padre, Guida, ed Amico!
Da questo momento, Io ti cedo i miei diritti sopra di essi: ti
supplico però di guardare con indulgenza i difetti, che l'occhio
parziale di Padre mi può aver celati, e di continuar loro
malgrado, la generosa tua Amicizia a chi tanto l'apprezza,
mentre sono di tutto Cuore.

Amico Carisimo   il tuo Sincersimo Amico
Vienna il p.mo Settembre 1785.

                                        W. A. Mozart

---

10   Mozart's dedication to Joseph Haydn, from the first published edition of the six
String Quartets (K.387, 421, 428, 458, 464 and 465) issued by Artaria and Co. as
'Op. X' on 19 September 1785.

Haydn had heard all the six Quartets (K.387, 421, 428, 458, 464, 465) which his younger friend had composed in his honour (he would subsequently dedicate them to him in print), on 14 January, the day on which Mozart completed the final work, K.465, and entered it in his Catalogue. We know of this from a letter Leopold wrote to his daughter in St Gilgen on 22 January 1785:[5]

[P.S.] This moment I have received 10 lines from your brother, in which he writes that his first subscription concert starts on the 11th of Feb. ..., that I should come soon, – that last Saturday he had his 6 Quartets, which he has sold to Artaria for 100 ducats, played to his dear friend Haydn and other good friends. At the end it says: 'Now I must sit down again at my concerto I've just begun [i.e. K.466, completed on 10 February (Catalogue)].'

Leopold Mozart now joined the Craft, and since he would be in Vienna for only a short period, his son's Lodge 'Zur Wohlthätigkeit' proposed Leopold and dispensed with much of the usual formality. Mozart *père* became an Entered Apprentice on 6 April, and on 16 April father and son are registered together, with their autograph signatures, at a meeting of 'Zur wahren Eintracht'; on this occasion Leopold was

11   The signatures of Leopold and Wolfgang Mozart (bracketed at right) on a protocol of the Viennese Lodge 'Zur wahren Eintracht', 16 April 1785, preserved in the Haus-, Hof- und Staatsarchiv, Vienna.

passed to the Fellow-Craft Degree 'with the usual ceremonies'. On the 22nd of that month, Leopold became a Master Mason at the 'Eintracht' Lodge under Ignaz von Born, and two days later father and son both attended the Lodge 'Zur gekrönten Hoffnung', where Ignaz von Born of the 'Eintracht' was honoured. In the course of the ceremonies, Wolfgang produced a new Cantata for the occasion, 'Die Maurerfreude' (K.471) for tenor, male choir and orchestra, the score of which was that same year published by the Viennese firm of Artaria and Co., Haydn's and Mozart's chief publishers. Other Masonic documents show us that Pasquale Artaria, one of the firm's founders, organized the engraving of the score; Artaria was a member of the 'Hoffnung' Lodge, and there exists a Masonic engraving of his portrait, dated 1785, which is now exhibited in the Museum of Freemasonry at Rosenau Castle (Lower Austria). Other Lodge Brethren contributed to the event: the tenor solo was sung by Valentin Adamberger, Mozart's first Belmonte in *Die Entführung*. Also, Wenzel Tobias Epstein, who was at various times an officer of the 'Hoffnung' Lodge and whose portrait we have recently discovered in his own commonplace book (now owned by the Historisches Museum der Stadt Wien), contributed the foreword to the printed score; we shall return to Epstein later. The income from the sale of copies of the Cantata – it was issued on 17 August 1785 – went to charity. The day after this ceremony, which had culminated in a splendid banquet (*Tafelloge*), Leopold Mozart left for Salzburg. His son was never to see him again.

Mozart's most important piece of Masonic music hitherto had originated in the deaths, within a day of each other in 1785, of two Brothers: Georg August, Duke of Mecklenburg-Strelitz (d. 6 November), and Franz, Count Esterházy of Galántha, Hungarian-Transylvanian Court Chancellor (d. 7 November). The Duke was an Honorary Member of the Lodge 'Zu den drei Adlern', the Count of the Lodge 'Zur gekrönten Hoffnung'; and it was in the latter that on 17 November 1785 was held a Lodge of Sorrows. Wenzel Tobias Epstein delivered the Oration (which was afterwards published, the proceeds of its sale being donated as usual for the benefit of the poor), while Mozart, using an extraordinary and fortuitous collection of musicians, some of

12   Valentin Adamberger, miniature portrait, *c.* 1785; present whereabouts unknown.

13   Title page of the published score (Vienna 1785) of Mozart's Cantata 'Die Maurerfreude' (K.471), the words of which were written by Franz Petran.

14, 15 *Left*: Georg August, Duke of Mecklenburg-Strelitz, anonymous oil painting (detail), *c.* 1769; present whereabouts unknown. *Right*: Franz, Count Esterházy, detail of a mezzotint by Franz Balko after J. G. Haid, 1769.

them travelling Brethren,[6] produced his *Maurerische Trauermusik* (K.477). This *Masonic Funeral Music*, with its heavy symbolism (concept of 'three'), also in its overall form (in the middle 'B' part there appears an old Gregorian chant, part of the music for Passion week),[7] reveals Mozart's total involvement with the theories and philosophies of death and their symbolic relationship to the First Degree of the Craft. In a famous letter to his father of 4 April 1787 – Leopold was then on his death-bed – Wolfgang writes:[8]

> As death, when we come to consider it closely, is the true goal of our existence, I have formed during the last few years such close relations with this best and truest friend of mankind, that his image is not only no longer terrifying to me, but is indeed very soothing and consoling! And I thank my God for graciously granting me the opportunity

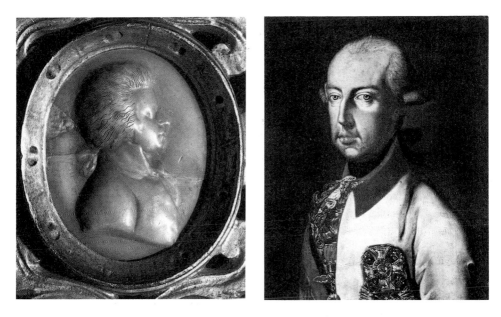

16, 17 *Left*: Wolfgang Amadeus Mozart, wax relief by an anonymous artist. *Right*: The Emperor Joseph II, by whom Mozart was appointed to serve as Court Chamber Musician in December 1785; anonymous portrait in oils (detail), *c.* 1790.

(you understand what I mean) of learning that death is the *key* which unlocks the door to our true happiness. I never lie down at night without reflecting that – young as I am – I may not live to see another day . . .

It was during the autumn of 1785 that Mozart began work, and completed in a period of some six weeks, the first draft of Le *nozze di Figaro*, which was first performed at the Burgtheater in Vienna on 1 May 1786. The Emperor Joseph II, encouraged by Lorenzo Da Ponte, was more or less directly responsible for the fact that the Opera could be given at all – the play by Beaumarchais, on which the libretto was based, was forbidden in the Austrian domains – and in 1787, Mozart was given a prestigious, though financially unrewarding, position as Court Chamber Musician to the Emperor. Several months before that

LA
FOLLE JOURNÉE,

OU LE

MARIAGE
DE FIGARO,

COMÉDIE EN CINQ ACTES
ET EN PROSE.

Par Mr. CARON de BEAUMARCHAIS.

Représentée, pour la premiere fois, à Paris par les Comédiens ordinaires du Roi, le 27 Avril 1784.

À PARIS, chez les Libraires associés.

M. DCC. LXXXV.

18   Title page of the first authorized French edition of the play by Beaumarchais on which the libretto of Mozart's Opera *Le nozze di Figaro* was based.

19   Mozart's autograph sketches for a Piano Concerto (Köchel/Einstein 467a), *c.*
1785; the page is remarkable for the many calculations in the composer's own hand.

official appointment (made on 6/7 December), an ominous note was
sounded by Leopold Mozart in a letter to his daughter Nannerl – the last
document we have from his pen, dated 28 May 1787: 'Your brother is
now living in the Landstraße no. 224. He does not say why he has
moved. Not a word. But unfortunately I can guess the reason.'[9] At this
time Mozart was beginning to get into debt, though exactly why and in
what circumstances he began living beyond his means remains a matter
for speculation.

23

In the summer of 1788, when Mozart was composing his last three Symphonies (K.543, 550, 551), his financial situation was getting steadily more desperate. Michael Puchberg, a member of the Lodge 'Zur Wahrheit' ('Truth') – see below – was lending Mozart a steady stream of money. We read:

Dearest Friend and Brother of the Order,

Owing to great difficulties and complications my affairs have become so involved that it is of the utmost importance to raise some money on these two pawnbroker's tickets. In the name of our friendship I implore you to do me this favour; but you must do it immediately. Forgive my importunity, but you know my situation ...[10]

This letter of 1788 was almost precisely contemporary with the composition of the G minor Symphony (K.550), completed on 25 July. A year later Mozart's situation had again deteriorated. In a letter to Michael Puchberg of 12 July 1789, we read:

... Good God! I am coming to you not with thanks but with fresh entreaties! Instead of paying my debts I am asking for more money! If you really know me, you must sympathize with my anguish at having to do so. I need not tell you once more that, owing to my unfortunate illness, I have been prevented from earning anything. But I must mention that, in spite of my wretched condition, I decided to give my subscription concerts at home in order to be able to meet at least my present great and frequent expenses, for I was absolutely convinced of your friendly assistance. But even this failed. Unfortunately Fate is so much against me, *though only in Vienna*, that even when I want to, I cannot make any money. A fortnight ago I sent round a list for subscribers and so far the only name on it is that of Baron van Swieten! ...[11]

Mozart was not the only one in trouble in Vienna in the 1780s. The Freemasons themselves were in a state of continuous crisis, and it had all been brought on by none other than the Emperor who, in a *Handbillet* of 11 December 1785, ordered that the number of Viennese Lodges – and,

20 The opening of the Finale of Mozart's Symphony No. 40 in G minor (K.550), from the autograph score completed in July 1788.

as we have seen, there were no less than eight of them be reduced to not more than three. Joseph II, it would seem, considered that the Masons in Vienna had become far too powerful. He wanted their numbers drastically reduced, and it was rather clever to force a reorganization within the Lodges so that many members felt obliged to resign, or simply no longer to attend. The Brethren themselves complied with this order earlier than required, and by 28 December 1785 the situation was as follows: the élite Lodge 'Zur wahren Eintracht', together with the 'Palmbaum' and 'Drei Adlern', constituted a new Lodge 'Zur Wahrheit'; the Lodge 'Zur gekrönten Hoffnung', Mozart's Lodge

'Zur Wohlthätigkeit' and the 'Drei Feuern' were fused into the principal Viennese Lodge 'Zur neugekrönten Hoffnung' ('New Crowned Hope'), which opened its doors for the first time on 14 January 1786. Both these new Lodges were voluntarily reduced to 180 members each. Two of the former Lodges, 'Zum heiligen Joseph' and 'Zur Beständigkeit', disappeared entirely, but some of their members joined 'New Crowned Hope'. Ignaz von Born was elected Master of the reconstituted Lodge 'Zur Wahrheit', but in August 1786 he resigned; Haydn simply stayed away from the new Lodge. The Emperor also demanded regular records of the Lodges, with precise lists of their members, whether present or absent, and, as a result of this supervision, many Lodge lists, both manuscript and printed, were incorporated into the 'Vertrauliche Akten' (Secret Files) of the Court Archives (Haus-, Hof- und Staatsarchiv), where they may be examined today.

We now come to the year 1790. On New Year's Eve 1789, Joseph Haydn – freshly arrived in Vienna from Eszterháza Castle (where he was still signing documents on 30 December) – was invited, together with Michael Puchberg, to a piano rehearsal of Mozart's new Opera, *Così fan tutte*. Mozart writes to Puchberg as follows:[1][2]

> ... Tomorrow on account of the appointment there can be nothing at our house. – I have too much work, – if you see Zisler anyway,

please tell him – Thursday [31 December], however, I invite you (but just you alone) to come at 10 o'clock in the morning to me, for a small opera rehearsal; – only you and Haydn are invited. – Then *a viva voce* I'll tell you about all the cabals of Salieri, which however came to naught – adieu

Always Your
thankful friend and Brother
W. A. Mozart

[Puchberg notes: 'sent 300 fl.']

Shortly afterwards, on 20 January 1790, Mozart writes to Michael Puchberg:[13]

... If you can and would trust me with another 100 fl., I should be very much indebted to you. –

Tomorrow is the first orchestral rehearsal in the theatre – Haydn will go with me – if your affairs allow of it, and if perhaps you would

22   The Burgtheater (right) in the Michaelerplatz, Vienna; engraving by Carl Schütz, 1783.

like to attend the rehearsal, you need only have the goodness to come to me tomorrow morning at 10 o'clock, and we will all go together.

Your most sincere friend
W. A. Mozart

20th January 1790
[Puchberg notes 'eodem sent the 100 fl.']

23   The First Violin part (intended for the leader of Haydn's orchestra, Luigi Tomasini) specially copied for the planned production of *Le nozze di Figaro* at Eszterháza which was cancelled following the death of Prince Nicolaus in September 1790; Esterházy Archives, Budapest.

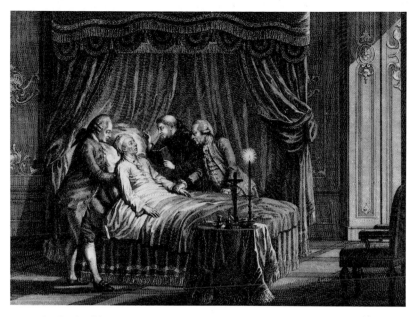

24   The death of the Emperor Joseph II; engraving by S. Mansfeld, 1790, published by Artaria and Co.

The actual performances of *Così fan tutte* at the Burgtheater took place on 26, 28 and 30 January – any or all of which Haydn could have attended – and then on 7 and 11 February. Emperor Joseph II died on 20 February. On 4 February Haydn had returned to Eszterháza, and in the middle of the month the opera season at Eszterháza began, naturally in the presence of Prince Nicolaus, now an old gentleman of seventy-five. And with the mention of Prince Nicolaus Esterházy, for whose entertainment incidentally Haydn was in this season of 1790 preparing a performance of Mozart's *Le nozze di Figaro* at Eszterháza Castle, we arrive at a startling and hitherto undiscovered relationship between Nicolaus Esterházy, Wolfgang Amadeus Mozart, the Freemasons and, specifically, the recently established Lodge 'Zur neugekrönten Hoffnung'.

In 1980 in Vienna, an elaborate exhibition commemorating the 200th anniversary of the death of the Empress Maria Theresa was mounted in Schönbrunn Castle. As part of that exhibition, there was a small section devoted to Freemasonry during her reign; one of the documents on display proved to be a small scholarly bombshell. It was a Lodge Protocol listing Prince Nicolaus Esterházy as Master of Ceremonies at 'Crowned Hope' (the 'new' now being tacitly omitted). Hitherto, modern scholars had no evidence that Esterházy had ever been a Freemason, much less an officer in a Viennese Lodge. In the course of the preparations for my illustrated volume *Haydn: a documentary study* (which Thames and Hudson published in 1981), examination of an enlarged photograph of a well-known but previously unidentified oil painting of a late eighteenth-century Austrian Lodge Ritual convinced me that the central figure in the foreground of that picture was (a) Master of Ceremonies and (b) Prince Nicolaus Esterházy, of whom many extant portraits are available for comparison.

Now this anonymous picture, owned by the Historisches Museum der Stadt Wien,[14] has always baffled the experts. It was agreed that it must represent a Viennese Lodge in the period we are considering, but no one had ever positively identified which one. First, a few words about the content of the picture. We see an oblong hall, the so-called Temple, its walls richly ornamented with designs and statues, the lighting provided by a central chandelier suspended on a cord, by candles in brackets on the wall, and by two sets of three candles at the far end of the room. This eastern part of the Temple, a dais raised above a set of three steps, includes the two 'altars' or pedestals of the principal officers of the Lodge. The allegorical painting seen in the background shows a body of water, with (on the left) the six-pointed Blazing Star, symbolic of the sun, and a rainbow; in biblical and Masonic language, the rainbow (which appeared after the Flood) is a sign of hope, hence it should have been clear from the symbolic meaning that the Lodge depicted was 'Crowned Hope'. Of the two pedestals at the eastern end, that on the left is for the Master (in German *Meister vom Stuhl*), here shown with his

25, 26 Central detail and (*overleaf*) the whole area of an anonymous oil painting showing a meeting of a Viennese Lodge, now restored and displayed in the Historisches Museum der Stadt Wien; scale of detail 1:2.

27–30 Portraits of Prince Nicolaus Esterházy. (*Above, left*) Detail of ill. 26, showing the Master of Ceremonies; actual size. (*Above, right*) Anonymous miniature showing the Prince in the uniform of an Austrian officer. (*Below, left*) Engraving by Ludwig Guttenbrunn, 1770 (detail). (*Below, right*) Anonymous portrait in oils (detail).

gavel raised. The book lying open on the table is probably the Bible, and one can distinguish a skull and, in front of it, a sword. To the right stands the pedestal of the Master's Deputy (*Deputierter Meister*), on which is a field-level, one of the basic Masonic symbols; of the three officers, the one on the right who is reading a document seems to be the Speaker (*Redner*). To the far right of the picture we see one of the Brother Servants who is in the process of raising the heavy curtains that close off the Temple. In the foreground a Candidate, his eyes bound (not yet having 'seen the light') and with hat in hand, is being initiated into the Craft. There are thirty-five Brethren present, some in military uniform, two clerics and several in national costumes. Across their chests they wear the Masonic square suspended, on either red or blue ribbons, around their necks – the different colours would seem to indicate two different Lodges, blue being of course the colour of St John. The Brethren wear Masonic aprons, either trimmed in blue and with blue rosettes against the usual white background, or with red trimmings.

In the autumn of 1926, this picture, then in bad condition, was offered to the Historisches Museum by the then owner, Rudolf von Tinti, whose family ancestors had been present at the Mozart quartet party mentioned above and had been members of the Viennese Lodge 'Zur wahren Eintracht'. The picture, then, came from a family with Masonic connections. It measures 80 × 100 cm., and has meanwhile been cleaned and restored. The late Otto Erich Deutsch, who published a reproduction of the picture, considered, wrongly, that it represented the Lodge 'Zur wahren Eintracht'. He adds that Mozart often visited the Lodge, as we have seen, as 'besuchender Bruder'. He then states, with a slight touch of irony, 'Readers steeped in fantasy will easily recognize him in the figure in the right foreground.'[15]

Once we had established that the Lodge portrayed was 'Crowned Hope' and that the Master of Ceremonies was Prince Nicolaus Esterházy, it was necessary to discover an authentic document in which Mozart, who was a member of the Lodge, is listed together with Prince Nicolaus. My wife has now found such a document, a complete Lodge Protocol of the year 1790 – see Appendix, pp. 65ff. – in which among the officers 'Niclas Eszterházy', member No. 19, is named as *Zeremonien Meister*; and listed among the 'Brethren Present' are not only Prince Nicolaus (No. 19) but also, as No. 56, 'Mozart Wolfgang k:k: Kapell Meister III [Degree]'. This previously unknown document is part of the 'Vertrauliche Akten' in the possession of the Haus-, Hof- und Staatsarchiv.

In determining Prince Nicolaus Esterházy's membership in the Lodge, all the available lists of the 'Crowned Hope' and 'New Crowned Hope' were examined, but from the very beginning, in 1786, when this new Lodge was grounded, to 1790, his name appears nowhere, in any capacity; whether he first entered the Craft in 1790, becoming Master of Ceremonies (which is unlikely), or whether he was previously a member and perhaps had his own Lodge in Eszterháza Castle, cannot now be determined. No list dated 1789 is known to have survived; but there exists a printed membership list, which, though undated, we are fortunately able to place in the year 1789. The Museum of Freemasonry in Rosenau Castle owns a Diploma issued to a member of 'Crowned Hope', one François Joseph de Bosset, dated 1789 and signed as follows: 'Fr: Jos. Bauernjöpel premier surveillant / Fr: Begontina grand maître / Fr. Wolf Maître député / Joseph Metz second surveillant / Fr. Fischer Secretaire'. By comparing these names with an undated printed membership list of present and absent Brothers in the Haus-, Hof- und Staatsarchiv, we find that they correspond exactly. The officers rotated each year; in 1789 Prince Nicolaus Esterházy was not yet a member and the position of Master of Ceremonies in that year was filled by Bro. Joseph Lepper, a factory owner. The most interesting fact about Mozart's Lodge 'Crowned Hope' was that in 1790 its members included several Esterházys. No less than four members of that illustrious family were Brethren: the Master was Johann, Count Esterházy, Royal Imperial Chamberlain, who had been the Lodge's Master in 1781 and would again fill that position in 1791.[16] As we have seen, the Master (Count Johann) stands at the eastern end of the Temple and holds the gavel of his office. Prince Nicolaus is the Master of Ceremonies. Another (the third) member is No. 17 of the 1790 list: he is given there as follows: '17. Eszterházy Franz S:Gr:v:k:k:

31 Extracts from a protocol of the Lodge 'Zur gekrönten Hoffnung' dated 1790, including the names of three members of the Esterházy family and Wolfgang Amadeus Mozart among the list of members present (*Anwesende Brüder*) – see Appendix, pp. 65ff.

Kämmerer III [Degree]'; this was Franz Seraphin, Count von Esterházy, a Master Mason, the son of Franz, Count Esterházy (who had been known as 'Quinquin') who had died in 1785 and was co-recipient of Mozart's *Maurerische Trauermusik* played in the Lodge of Sorrows. Franz Seraphin followed in his father's footsteps as *Hofrat* (Count Councillor) in the Transylvanian-Hungarian Court Chancellery. To the far left in the painting one sees a distinguished, hook-nosed gentleman in a travelling great-coat who seems to be observing the ritual as an onlooker rather than as a participant (ill. 35). What can be the explanation of this curious state of affairs? We believe this Brother to be Johann Nepomuk, Count von Esterházy, who is listed in 1790 as No. 30 of the absent Brethren and as a Master Mason and 'k: k: Kämmerer und Gub: Rath zu Hermannstadt'; in other words, he was not among the assembled Lodge because he had been called away to Hermannstadt in Transylvania where he was Administrator of the Province. We have

34 Detail (actual size) from the right foreground in ill. 26.

32 Mozart, plaster medallion by L. Posch, 1788–9, height 8·2 cm; displayed in the house in Salzburg in which the composer was born.

33 Mozart, plaster cast by or after L. Posch, 1788–9, here shown reversed left to right for comparison with the profile seen in ill. 34.

35–37 Johann Nepomuk, Count Esterházy. Detail of the standing figure on the left in ill. 26, with for comparison details from two known portraits of the Count: an engraving by Adam Ehrenreich (*above*) and a lithograph by F. Lütgendorff, published in 1827.

two contemporary portraits available for comparison (ills. 36, 37).

The officers of the 1790 list are given as follows, under 'Dignitaries and Officers': Master was Count Johann Esterházy; his Deputy, Joseph von Metz (a member of the Dutch Section in the government); 'Erster Aufseher' (Warden) was Bro. Joseph Bauernjöpl, 'Kanzelist b[ey] d[en] ver[einigten] Hofstellen'; 'Zweiter Aufseher' was Franz Eugen, Count von Traun und Abensperg, Royal Imperial Chancellor; Secretary was Karl Fischer von Ehrenbach, Councillor of Legation of the Sachsen-Koburgs; the Speaker was Anton Niering von Lövenfels, described as 'Konzepist b[ey] d[er] geistl[ichen] Hofkom[m]ission'; Treasurer ('Schatz Meister') was Johann Nepomuk von Török from the Imperial Royal War Ministry's Bookkeeping Department; and of course Prince Nicolaus Esterházy was Master of Ceremonies.

In the painting the right-hand group includes two clerics (ill. 40). The Abbot in white robes can only be No. 38 among the absentees of our surviving 1790 list, Johann Lambert von Hanotte, 'Kanonik[us] und Prälat zu Huy in Lüttich'. He was Abbot at Huy (Huey), a monastery of the Augustinian Canons near Liège (Lüttich) who, unlike the Austrian branch of the order, still wore an all-white habit (in Austria it was white and black). Further along is a Franciscan or Capuchin monk in a brown habit; this figure caused, initially, enormous difficulty as to identification, for there is no monk of either Order listed anywhere in the Lodge protocols. But a recent discovery made in the Historisches Museum has perhaps unravelled this Gordian knot. One of the members of the 'Crowned Hope' Lodge was Johann Georg Kronauer, a teacher of languages, who kept a commonplace book which is now in the department of manuscripts of the Austrian National Library; this book is famous because, among other Brethren, Mozart signed it, with the following: 'Patience and tranquillity of mind contribute more to cure our distempers as [*sic*] the whole art of medicine. – Wien den 30tn März 1787. Ihr wahrer aufrichtiger Freund und O[rdens] Br[uder] Wolfgang Amadeus Mozart Mitglied der sehr E[hrenwerten] □ zur Neugekrönten Hofnung [*sic*] im O[rient] v[on] W[ien]' (facsimile in Deutsch, *Mozart und seine Welt . . .*, p. 206). Now

41

38, 39 *Above*: Silhouette of Johann Georg Kronauer, from a commonplace book (formerly owned by Gabriele von Baumberg). *Below*: A page from a commonplace book kept by Kronauer, including a silhouette of Pater Ignaz Faber. Historisches Museum der Stadt Wien (cf. p. 63).

42

40 Detail of ill. 26 (actual size), showing the two clerics present: the Abbot in a white habit, identified as Johann Lambert von Hanotte; and, second from left, a monk in a brown habit, possibly Pater Ignaz Faber of the Franciscan Order.

this Kronauer, a silhouette of whom has survived from a lost *Liber amicorum*,[17] kept *another* volume of his commonplace book. The part in the Austrian National Library begins with the year 1783. The newly discovered volume in the Historisches Museum is obviously the National Library volume's predecessor, up to 1783. On page 53v. we find the silhouette of a Capuchin monk named Ignace Faber; there are Masonic symbols surrounding his portrait, and he has written above it, 'vera effigies ad vivum expressa in statu corruptionis suae', and on the adjoining page (54) Pater Faber has written his 'Protestatio / Donatoris' in Latin and German verses, signed 'Wien den 7:ᵗⁿ decemb / 1781

Opposite

42, 43 Portraits of known members of the Lodge 'Zur gekrönten Hoffnung' whose names appear in the 1790 protocol: (*right*) Philipp, *Freiherr* von Vukassevich, engraved by J. H. Löschenkohl; and (*left*) Ludwig, Count von Lehrbach, shown in an anonymous silhouette.

41 Detail of ill. 26, (actual size), showing a senior military officer, identified from the 1790 Lodge protocol as Ferdinand, Count Harrach.

Votre tres-humble serviteur et ami / P: Francisevis Ignace Faber / de l'ordre de Saint Fransevis / des Peres Capucins de la Province du Franconie.' We submit that this unorthodox Pater Faber may have been the clerical visitor portrayed in this Masonic group.

Among the army officers portrayed, one is shown as part of a group of two, standing between the Lodge officers in the eastern niche and the seated group with their backs to the viewer. He is an officer of a very

senior rank, and among the Brethren present in the 1790 list one name fits perfectly: No. 34, Ferdinand, Count Harrach, Lieutenant Field-Marshal and the owner of a Cavalry Regiment. After 1786, the members of this Regiment No. 21, formerly Cuirassiers, wore a white jacket with dark-blue facings and white buttons, and white knee-breeches. A General would always wear a red waistcoat and red knee-breeches, his white jacket would have red facings; but when inspecting his own regiment as its Colonel he would wear a colonel's uniform with dark-blue facings. In the Lodge, however, this Brother would have probably worn the General's uniform.[18]

Among the absent Brethren we have listed as No. 107, Philipp, *Freiherr* von Vukassevicz (Vukassevich), Knight of the Theresa Order and Lieutenant-Colonel, of whom a portrait by the celebrated engraver J. H. Löschenkohl survives. And moving from the military to civilian absentees, we have corroboratory pictorial evidence of list No. 62, Ludwig, Count von Lehrbach, Privy Councillor at the Court and Commissary at the *Reichsversammlung* at Ratisbon (Regensburg).

Opposite

44   Detail of ill. 26 (actual size) showing the seated group in the left foreground.

45   Detail from an engraved portrait of the publisher Ignaz Alberti; a definite resemblance can be seen between this portrait and the second figure from the left in ill. 44.

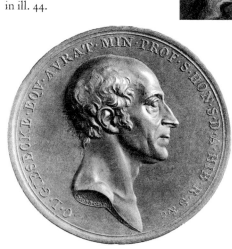

46   Karl Ludwig Giesecke (d. 1833), depicted on a medallion by W. S. Mossop; the fourth figure from the left in ill. 44 may perhaps be this actor and singer, who was active in Vienna at the period when the Masonic group was painted.

We have, moreover, portraits of several other members listed as present on the 1790 list of 'Crowned Hope':

(1) Ignatz (Ignaz) Alberti, No. 3, engraver and printer. May we see him, with his generous and rather feminine mouth, in the second man seated to the left of our picture?

(2) Karl Ludwig Giesege (Giesecke), whose real name was Metzler, an actor and singer who was a member of the Schikaneder Company at the Freyhaus-Theater and who was the First Slave in

47

47, 48 Two known members of the Lodge 'Zur gekrönten Hoffnung': (*right*) Carlo Mechetti, engraving by David Weiss after Ferracuti; and Christian Friedrich Wappler, engraving by Jakob Adam – possibly the penultimate seated figure in ill. 49.

Opposite
49 Detail of ill. 26 (actual size), showing the seated group in the left background.

Mozart's *Die Zauberflöte* in 1791. Later he emigrated to Ireland where he became Professor of Mineralogy at the University of Dublin; in a book published in Hamburg in 1849, Giesecke is said to have claimed at least part-authorship of the libretto to *Die Zauberflöte*.[19] Whatever the truth of that assertion, Giesecke was an interesting man, and perhaps we may identify him as the fourth Brother in the left-hand seated group. In the 1790 list he appears at No. 26 (described as 'actor').

(3) Carlo Mechetti, listed at No. 54 as 'without occupation', later became a well-known publisher. In view of the fact that the painting has been restored and cleaned (a necessity in view of the bad condition in

which it was delivered to the Historisches Museum), one hesitates to attempt any further firm identifications except in the case of

(4) Christian Friedrich Wappler (list No. 83), publisher and literary man in Vienna. We believe him to be the penultimate Brother in the left-hand group, or rather seated behind the standing officer.

Wenzel Tobias Epstein, a colourful and interesting Brother whose *Liber amicorum* in the Historisches Museum[20] fortunately contains his portrait made at Venice in 1784, is listed as absent in the years 1789 and 1790 (in the 1790 protocol he is No. 29, described as Secretary of Gubernatorial Rank in Innsbruck); he had recently been raised to the

50, 51   Wenzel Tobias Epstein, portrayed in a drawing by Francesco Galimberti, 1784; compare the features with the standing figure to the right of the Candidate in ill. 26, seen in the detail (*right*).

nobility and was now Ep(p)stein von Ankersberg. Although officially listed as absent, at least in this one 1790 protocol, it seems possible that we have his portrait in the group, standing next to Nicolaus Esterházy. The turned-up nose and sparkling eyes agree with the authentic 1784 pen-and-ink drawing (ill. 50). It is believed that the function of this Brother, one of the two standing by the Candidate, is one known in those days as 'le frère terrible' ('schreckliche Bruder'), a Brother who represented the terrors and punishment that await the newly initiated Mason should he reveal the Lodge's (and Craft's) secrets. It must be repeated that only one Lodge list of 'Crowned Hope' in 1790 is available, and it is quite possible that in another such list of about this period, one might have found Epstein von Ankersberg listed as present. (His function as 'frère terrible' is one involved only with the ritual associated with initiation to the First Degree, and in that capacity he would not have been listed among the Lodge officers.)

And now a few words about the painting's date, which we may suggest on the basis of the whereabouts of one of the Lodge's most illustrious members, Prince Nicolaus Esterházy. In 1789, Prince Nicolaus was not yet a member of the Lodge 'Zur gekrönten Hoffnung', as we have been able to establish (*supra*). From sources in the Esterházy Archives and in the Haydn literature, we know that in the early part of 1790 Haydn left Vienna for Eszterháza, to be precise, on 4 February,[20] and that in the middle of that month opera performances, in the presence of Prince Nicolaus, started at Eszterháza. Prince Nicolaus died at Vienna on 28 September 1790; he had arrived there in the early days of that month. It is unlikely, if he were a dying man, that he would have attended the Lodge in September, and therefore we may deduce that the picture must have been painted in the year 1790, probably between 1 January and 15 February.

Why was the picture painted? To preserve the record of a famous Viennese Lodge? As a strictly accurate portrayal of a Masonic ceremony, some aspects strike one as curious. In the first place, it would seem that at least three events are depicted as taking place simultaneously. In the east of the Temple, the Speaker is reading a document and the Master is wielding his gavel; in the middle left, a senior army officer seems to be in ritual contact with another Brother, while, in the centre foreground, a Candidate is being welcomed into the Lodge. These events would hardly take place simultaneously, however, in the normal course of a Lodge meeting. The next matter that seems curious, to say the least, is that three groups of Brethren are busy talking with one another: in the left-hand group the first two Brethren are in conversation, and the next two seem also to be engrossed in a discussion (ill. 44); surely, however, our attention is, and was meant to be, drawn to Mozart, in a prominent place, pictorially, seated at the end of the right-hand group of Brethren (ill. 52); and he too is deep in conversation with an elderly gentleman who, with Brother Nicolaus Esterházy, would seem to be the oldest of the whole group. Is it our imagination, or does Mozart's neighbour, whose left hand seems to be raised in protest, look faintly shocked by what the composer is saying? And there can be no doubt whatever that the third Brother in that column is taking a pinch of snuff, the snuff-box being held, in fraternal fashion, by his companion to the right. Do we not detect, too, in that fourth Brother of the column, a surprised and slightly amused (or shocked?) glance directed towards the chattering Mozart?

We do not wish to trespass on the quasi-sacred right of art historians to speculate upon the paintings they are investigating, and in any case to do so with the scene depicted involves too many hypothetical queries which can hardly, in present circumstances, be anwered. But we submit that there are certain overtones in the picture which suggest that the content and message are perhaps more obscure and involved than has hitherto been imagined. Further research and new discoveries will perhaps make it possible to analyze in greater depth the history and content of this Masonic group – presumably painted by an as yet unidentified Brother.

In conclusion, let us return to the central figure – Mozart – and his Masonic connections in the last year of his life. In 1791, Mozart went on to compose *Die Zauberflöte*, the libretto was by Emanuel Schikaneder, who had been a member of a Lodge at Ratisbon (Regensburg) but is not listed in any of the lodge protocols in Vienna. In this connection, we might quote from a letter by the Viennese composer (and reputedly a pupil of Mozart), Ignaz von Seyfried (1776–1841), to Friedrich Treitschke, who collaborated with Beethoven in 1814.[21]

> ... Schikaneder's personal acquaintance with Mozart ... was in a Freemasons' Lodge – but actually not that famous one of Born ['Zur wahren Eintracht'], to which are supposed to have belonged Vienna's first dignitaries and the élite of the literary world of that era – rather a so-called private or banqueting Lodge ['eine sogenannte Winkel- oder Freß-Loge'], where in weekly evening meetings one diverted oneself with gambling, music and the many joys of a well appointed table, as Gieseke [*sic*] often told me ...

The composition of *Die Zauberflöte* was interrupted by the Coronation ceremonies in Prague in early September 1791, in which the new Emperor, Leopold II, was crowned King of Bohemia, and for which occasion Mozart contributed his last Italian Opera, *La clemenza*

52   Detail of ill. 26, showing Mozart and the group on his right.

Emanuel Schikaneder

Almanach
für
Theaterfreunde
auf das
Jahr 17 91.
Wien, bey Mathias Ludwig in
der Singerstraße.

I. Albrecht sc.

53, 54 Frontispiece portrait of the impresario Emanuel Schikaneder and title page showing the Freyhaus-Theater, Vienna, from the *Almanach für Theaterfreunde 1791*, engraved by Ignaz Albrecht; and (*left*) a portrait of Schikaneder engraved by J. H. Löschenkohl.

55   The unfinished portrait of Mozart, painted by his brother-in-law Joseph Lange, 1789–90; the artist's intention was to show the composer seated at the keyboard.

56–58 Vignettes of clasped hands and (*opposite, below*) chain symbolic of the brotherhood of Freemasonry, as expressed in the words of the *Kettenlied* (*opposite, above*) sung at the closing of the Lodge 'Zur gekrönten Hoffnung'. These items are taken from a print of the *Kettenlied* sung at the St John Lodges in Vienna in 1782. The music is from the first edition of the Cantata, K.623, where it appears as an Appendix.

di Tito. The first performance of *Die Zauberflöte*, at the Freyhaus-Theater an der Wieden, took place on Friday, 30 September 1791. Mozart was now in the early stages of the *Requiem*, which of course he left unfinished, but he had time to complete, about 7 October, the Clarinet Concerto in A, K.622, for Anton Stadler.[22] The final completed work which he entered in his thematic catalogue is dated 15 November 1791: 'Eine kleine freymaurer-kantate' (Little Masonic Cantata), K.623. The text is said to be by Schikaneder, but when the work was issued by the Lodge after Mozart's death, the announcement noted 'the words are the work of a member' [of the Lodge 'Zur gekrönten Hoffnung']; as we have just seen, however, Emanuel Schikaneder was *not* a member of that Lodge. This same announcement, which was printed in the *Wiener Zeitung* on 25 January 1792, informs us that Mozart 'himself conducted the performance in the circle of his best friends two days before his final illness.'[23] The text clearly refers to the inauguration of a new Temple, and in the announcement it is stated that the Cantata was for 'the inauguration of a Masonic Lodge'. We have, moreover,

The words of the *Kettenlied* read:

Zum Schluß der □

Laßt uns mit geschlungnen Händen,	Es umschlänge diese Kette
Brüder, diese Arbeit enden	Es wie diese heil'ge Stätte
Unter frohem Jubelschall	Auch den ganzen Erdenhall.

evidence from Constanze Mozart, talking to Vincent and Mary Novello in Salzburg in 1829. Mary Novello's Diary[24] informs us: '(July 17th) ... [He] wrote a Masonic ode which so delighted the company for whom it was written that he returned quite elated; "Did I not know that I have written better, I should think this the best of my work," [said Mozart] ...'.

59   The house in which Mozart died, from a watercolour by E. Hutter, 1847.

60   Title page of the Oration delivered by Karl Philipp Hensler at a Lodge of Sorrows held following the death of Mozart, as published by Ignaz Alberti in 1792; this is the only known surviving copy.

MAURERREDE
AUF
MOZARTS TOD.

VORGELESEN

BEY EINER

MEISTERAUFNAHME

IN DER

SEHR EHRW. ST. JOH.

ZUR

GEKRÖNTEN HOFFNUNG

IM ORIENT VON WIEN

VOM

B^{dr.} H . . . . r.

WIEN,

GEDRUCKT BEYM BR. IGNAZ ALBERTI.

1792.

After a short illness, the last stages of which were characterized by renal failure, Mozart died, at fifty-five minutes past midnight, on 5 December 1791. The Masons held a Lodge of Sorrows in his memory, and the Oration was printed by Ignaz Alberti, a member of Mozart's own Lodge, who had also published the first libretto of *Die Zauberflöte*.[25] Mozart's earthly remains were given the last rites in front of the Kruzifix-Kapelle of St Stephen's Cathedral at three-o'clock in the afternoon of 6 December 1791 and thereupon taken to St Marx Cemetery outside the city walls, there to be placed in an unmarked grave.

NOTES

For full details of works cited see Bibliography, p. 63.

1 O. E. Deutsch, *Mozart Dokumente*, p. 204.
2 'In Eminenti Apostolatus', issued by Pope Clement XII.
3 In the Stefan Zweig Collection (owned by Mrs Eva Alberman, London); since 1957 on permanent loan to the British Museum (British Library); a facsimile was issued in Vienna in the 1930s. The title reads: 'Verzeichnüß aller meiner Werke vom Monath Febrario 1784 bis Monath [. . .] 1 [. . .]'.
4 O. E. Deutsch (with Wilhelm A. Bauer), *Mozart – Briefe und Aufzeichnungen*, III, p. 373.
5 Op. cit., p. 368.
6 There were present, this autumn, two travelling Brethren, Anton David and Vincenz Springer, who played the basset horn; they later turn up in London in 1791, playing at a Haydn-Salomon concert. Presumably Mozart's friend Anton Stadler played clarinet (for this Brother, Mozart composed the Clarinet Concerto in A, K.622), while the double-bassoon part was played by one Theodor Lotz (or Locz). Masonic concert programmes of the period have survived in which these Brethren appeared (20 October and 15 December; see Deutsch, *Mozart Dokumente*, pp. 223 and 226).
7 Also used by Haydn in his Symphony No. 26 in D minor ('Lamentatione'), c. 1768, and elsewhere.
8 Emily Anderson, *The Letters of Mozart and his Family*, II, p. 907.
9 Op. cit., p. 908n.
10 Op. cit., p. 917.

11 Op. cit., p. 930.
12 O. E. Deutsch, *Mozart – Briefe und Aufzeichnungen*, IV, p. 100.
13 Op. cit., p. 102.
14 Inv. no. 47.927.
15 O. E. Deutsch, 'Innenansicht einer Wiener Freinmaurer-Loge', *Wiener Schriften* 5 (1957), pp. 96ff.
16 In *Mozart und seine Welt in zeitgenössichen Bildern* (Kassel 1961), by O. E. Deutsch – illustration 448 (p. 211) and explanation (p. 349), we read: 'Johann Nepomuk, Count Esterházy (1754–1840) – The chamberlain was Master of the "Crowned Hope" Lodge in 1781, and from 1790 to 1791 he was Master of the "New Crowned Hope", Mozart's last Lodge . . .'. Professor Deutsch has confused Count Johann with Count Johann Nepomuk.
17 Formerly owned by the Austrian poet Gabriele von Baumberg; Historisches Museum der Stadt Wien, 110.989 (84.903). The first volume of the Kronauer *Liber amicorum* is in the same museum, 124.508.
18 This military information was kindly supplied by Dr Günther Dirrheimer of the Heeresgeschichtliches Museum in the Arsenal, Vienna, in January 1982. Dr Dirrheimer also noted that, according to the 1790 attendance list, the following military men could be identified among those present. Prince Nicolaus Esterházy (No. 19) had been since 1753 owner of Infantry Regiment No. 33. If in uniform, he would have worn a white jacket with dark-blue facings on the collar and sleeves, and white buttons. No. 33:

Guepferd Valentin, army doctor, his uniform was a light-blue jacket, red waistcoat and breeches, black facings, yellow buttons. No. 38: Philipp, *Edler* von Holbeinsberg, Major in the 'Bellegrini' (*recte*: Pellegrini) Regiment of Infantry; from 1767 grey facings with white buttons. No. 77: Johann Stark, *Oberlieutnant* (First Lieut.) in the Infantry Regiment Carl Toscana No. 3; blue facings, white buttons. No. 79: Joseph, Count Thun, Captain of the Prussian Infantry, since 1771 Infantry Regiment No. 24; dark-blue facings and white buttons.

Among the absent Brethren, he noted the following. No. 1: Philipp von Balthaser, First Lieutenant of the Nassau Cuirassiers, from 1782 attached to Cavalry Regiment No. 14; bright-blue facings with white buttons. No. 16: Karl, Count von Clouair Briant, Captain with the Regiment Carl Toscana; cf. Johann Stark No. 77, above. No. 19: Joseph Danoz, Captain with the Ingenieur (Engineers); blue jacket with cherry-red facings, straw-coloured (*paille*) waistcoat and breeches. No. 21: Karl Derbey, First Lieutenant with the Engineers; No. 19, above. No. 42: Philipp Count Heister, Lieutenant-Colonel with the Infantry Regiment 'Gommingen' (*recte*: Gemmingen-Hornberg), from 1778 Infantry Regiment No. 21; sea-green facings, yellow buttons. No. 48: Wenzel, *Freiherr* von Kapaun, *Rittmeister* with the Harrach Cuirassiers; see text *re* Ferdinand, Count Harrach. No. 49: Joseph Keller, Grenadier Lieutenant with the Kaunitz Infantry, from 1784 owned by Wenzel Anton, Prince Kaunitz; crab-red facings and white buttons. No. 52: Franz, Count von Khevenhüller, Lieutenant with the Ligne Infantry, from 1770 owned by Carl de Ligne; grey facings, yellow buttons (Regiment No. 30). No.

61: Ferdinand, Count Laurenzin d'Ormond, Lieutenant with Archduke Franz Cavalry, from 1788 Cuirassier Regiment No. 29 belonging to the Archduke; white jacket, black facings, white buttons. No. 68: Franz von De la Marino, Grenadier Captain in the Imperial Infantry Regiment No. 1; wine-red (*Pompadour-rot*) facings, yellow buttons. No. 88: Ludwig von Rheday, Lieutenant with the Wurmser Hussars, Regiment No. 30, owned by General Wurmser since 1775; hussar's jacket (dolman) with fur trimmings and a so-called shako (Hungarian, *csákó*) hat in 'parrot-green' colour. No. 98: Philipp, Count von Starhemberg, *Oberstwachtmeister* (first sergeant-major of cavalry), from 1757 this position known as *Charge Major*. No. 99: Karl Leopold, Count Steim, owner of an Infantry Regiment since 1773 (dissolved in 1809); violet facings, white buttons. No. 103: Samuel, Count Teleky, *Rittmeister* with the Nassau Cuirassiers; light-blue facings, white buttons.

19 The pertinent section is quoted in Deutsch, *Dokumente*, p. 475.

20 His letter to Maria Anna von Genzinger; Landon, *Haydn at Eszterháza*, pp. 736f.

21 Deutsch, *Dokumente*, pp. 471f.

22 Mozart writes to his wife Constanze, on Friday, 7 October 1791 (*Briefe und Aufzeichnungen*, IV, 157): '... then I orchestrated almost the whole rondo [of the Concerto] for Stadler, and meanwhile there came a letter from Stadler in Prague ...'.

23 Deutsch, *Mozart und die Wiener Logen*, pp. 16f.

24 *A Mozart Pilgrimage*, p. 125.

25 Facsimilie of the address given at the Lodge of Sorrows: O. E. Deutsch in the *Schweizerische Musikzeitung* (February 1956). There is also a facsimile of the first libretto of *Die Zauberflöte*, Wiener Bibliophilen-Gesellschaft, Vienna 1942.

SELECT BIBLIOGRAPHY

Manuscript Sources

(1) Haus-, Hof- und Staatsarchiv, Vienna:
Vertrauliche Akten, Karton 72 (alt 114); Karton 70 (alt 110–111); Karton 74 (alt 116); Karton 77 (alt 120–122); Karton 98: Verzeichnis sämtlicher Logen für die Landesloge in Wien, 1785.

(2) Historisches Museum der Stadt Wien:
[*Liber amicorum* (1779–91) of Wenzel Tobias Epstein (1757–1824)], inv. no. 56.192, 217 pp., 10·5 × 17 cm.
[*Liber amicorum* (1779–83), probably of Johann Georg Kronauer], inv. no. 124.508; 11·6 × 19 cm. Probably vol. I; vol. II is in the Handschriftensammlung of the Österreichische Nationalbibliothek, Cod. S.n. 4832. Translation (Franz Bernhart), in *Ars Quatuor Coronatorum* (*Transactions of the Quatuor Coronati Lodge*), 5 Oct. 1956, Margate.
[*Liber amicorum*, lost (disappeared 1945) of Gabriele von Baumberg (1766–1839), but photograph of silhouette of Johann Georg Kronauer extant, inv. no. 84.903.]

(3) Schloß Rosenau, Lower Austria:
Large collection of Masonic artefacts and documents on permanent exhibition. Also documents from the Historisches Museum der Stadt Wien: Diploma of the Lodge 'Zur gekrönten Hoffnung' of 1789, inv. no. 53.429; of 1791, inv no. 31.620.

Printed Sources

Short titles of these works, as used in the text, will be easily recognizable as such.

Journal für Freymaurer. Eine Festschrift der Grossloge von Österreich zum 250. Jahrestag der Gründung der Englischen Grossloge, Vienna, 1967 (with articles in German and English).

Schloßmuseum Rosenau: *Österreichische Freimaurerlogen: Humanität und Toleranz im 18. Jahrhundert*. Catalogue of the Museum at Rosenau Castle, Lower Austria, 1976.

[ANDERSON, EMILY:] *The Letters of Mozart and his Family*, Chronologically arranged, translated and edited by E. A. (2nd ed., A. H. King and M. Carolan), 2 vols., London 1966.

BERNHART, FRANZ: 'Freemasonry in Austria – A short historical Sketch', in *Ars Quatuor Coronatorum* (*Transactions of the Quatuor Coronati Lodge*), 1962, pp. 1ff.

DEUTSCH, OTTO ERICH:

(1) *Mozart und die Wiener Logen*, Zur Geschichte seiner Freimaurer-Komposition, Herausgegeben von der Großloge von Wien, Vienna 1932

(2) *Mozart – Die Dokumente seines Lebens*, Kassel 1961 (Serie X, Supplement, Werkgruppe 34, Neue Ausgabe sämtlicher Werke).

(3) 'Innenansicht einer Wiener Freimaurer-Loge', *Wiener Schriften* 5 (1957), pp. 96ff.

(4) [with Wilhelm A. Bauer:] *Mozart – Briefe und Aufzeichnungen, Gesamtausgabe*, 7 vols., Kassel 1962–75.

LANDON, H. C. ROBBINS: *Haydn, Chronicle and Works: Haydn at Eszterháza 1766–1790*, London and Bloomington, Ind., 1978.

[NOVELLO, MARY and VINCENT:] *A Mozart Pilgrimage, Being the Travel Diaries of Vincent and Mary Novello in the year 1829*. Transcribed and compiled by Nerina Medici di Marignano, edited by Rosemary Hughes; London 1955.

SMYTH, FREDERICK: 'Brother Mozart of Vienna', *Ars Quatuor Coronatorum* (*Transactions of the Quatuor Coronati Lodge*), 1974, pp. 37ff.

ACKNOWLEDGEMENTS

I should like to thank the following institutions and individuals for their help in supplying information and photographs for use in research and as illustrations (as noted below):

The Albertina, Vienna (ill. 22); the Austrian National Tourist Office, London (ills. 32, 55); the Trustees of the British Library (ills. 5, 6); the Freimaurerisches Museum, Schloß Rosenau, Lower Austria; the Gesellschaft der Musikfreunde, Vienna (ills. 7, 8, 20); the Haus-, Hof- und Staatsarchiv, Vienna (ills. 11, 31); the Heeresgeschichtliches Museum, Arsenal, Vienna; the Historisches Museum der Stadt Wien (ills. 26, 38, 39, 42, 43, 47, 50); the Hummel Archives, Florence (now Goethe-Museum, Düsseldorf; ill. 33); the Mozarteum, Salzburg (ills. 9, 19); the National Széchényi Library (Országos Széchényi Könyvtár), Budapest (ill. 23); the Handschriftensammlung and the Bildarchiv of the Österreichische National-bibliothek, Vienna (ills. 36, 45, 46, 48, 53, 54, 60); Altgraf Salm, Schloß Steyeregg, Upper Austria (ill. 28); the Museo della Scala, Milan (ill. 16); the Stadtbibliothek, Vienna; Mr John Webb, of the Order of St John, London; and my wife, Else Radant Landon, who did a great deal of research on my behalf and also put at my disposal her invaluable photographic archives.

H. C. R. L.

APPENDIX

'List of members of the Correct and Complete St John □ "Crowned Hope" in the Orient of Vienna. 5790 [1790]'; Vienna, Haus-, Hof- und Staatsarchiv, Vertrauliche Akten 114 (new: Karton 72). Roman numerals on the right indicate the First (Entered Apprentice), Second (Fellow-Craft) or Third (Master Mason) Degree, appropriate to each Brother.

Verzeichnis der Mitglieder der gerechten und vollkommenen St: Johannes □ zur gekrönten Hofnung [sic] im Orient von Wien. 5790.

Dignitärs und Beamte
Meister vom Stuhl Br: Johann Eszterhazy Nr. 18
Deputirter Meister Br: Metz Nr. 55
Erster Aufseher Br: Bauernjöpl Nr. 8
Zweiter Aufseher Br: Traun u. Abensperg Nr. 80
Sekretär Br: Fischer v. Ehrenbach Nr. 22
Redner Br: Niering v. Löwenfels Nr. 59
Schatz Meister Br: Török Nr. 81
Zeremonien Meister Br: Niclas Eszterhazy Nr. 19

Anwesende Brüder

1.	Aichelburg Cajet. Gr. v.	k.k. Rait Off: bei d. Güt: Zentral Hofbuchhaltg.	III
2.	Aichham[m]er Alois Ant:	Kanzlist und Hw: Br: F. v. Dietrichstein	III
3.	Alberti Ignaz	Kupferstecher u. Buchdrucker	III
4.	Ankermüller Emanuel	Expedits Adjunct b.d. k k ver: Hofstellen	III
5.	Antoin Joh: Baptist	Offizial im niederl. Depart.	III
6.	Ballogh Jos: von	der Arzneikunde Doktor	III
7.	Barth Franz Xav:[er]	d. Arzneikunde Doktor	III
8.	Bauernjöpl Jos:	Kanzlist b.d. ver. Hofstellen	III
9.	Begontina Joh: von	d. Arzneikunde Doktor	III
10.	Benisch Franz Xav:[er]	k:k: Sekretär	III
11.	Braunrasch Franz	k:k: Hof Agent	III
12.	Cantz Franz	Weltpriester u. Pfarrer auf d. Wieden	III
13.	Caron Karl Philipp	Privat Erzieher	III
14.	Cristan Thomas	d. Arzneikunde Doktor	III
15.	Colombazzo Vittorino	Tonkünstler	III

16.	Dischendorfer Franz	Privat Gelehrter	III
17.	Eszterhazy Franz S[eraphin]: Gr: v:	k:k: Kämmerer	III
18.	Eszterhazy Joh: Graf	k:k: Kämmerer	III
19.	Eszterhazy Nik: Fürst	k:k: Kämmerer	III
20.	Ezelt v. Lövenfels Ignatz	Handelsmann	III
21.	Ehle Gebhard	Graveur	III
22.	Fischer v. Ehrenbach Karl	Sachsen Koburgl. Legaz. Rath	III
23.	Fischer v. Riselbach Adalb:	Protokollist b.d. Banc: Direction	II
24.	Geley Michael	der Arzneikunde Doktor	I
25.	Gerubell Johann	Stallmeister beim B. Ant: Eszterhazy	I
26.	Giesege Karl Ludwig	Schauspieler	I
27.	Giegleitner Franz	Interesssent und Direkteur der mähr. Neustädter Wollenfabrik	II
28.	Giuliani Leopold von	Hofsekretär b.d.k.k. geh: Hof und Staats Kanzlei italienischen Departement	III
29.	Glaser Joh: Nep:	Raitrath bei der k:k: Stiftungen Hof Buchhalterei	III
30.	Gräffer Rudolf	Buchhändler	III
31.	Groschmidt Franz Xaver v.	k:k: Sekretär	III
32.	Gruber Karl	Offiziant bei d. Banc: Gefällen Administr.	III
33.	Guepferd Valentin	Staabs Chirurgus	III
34.	Harrach Ferd: Gr. von	k:k: Kämmerer, Feld Marschall-Lieutenant und Innhaber eines Kav: Regiments	III
35.	Herzog Joseph	Fabrik Innhaber	I
36.	Hirt Ferdinand	Erzieher des jung: F: Lobkowitz	II
37.	Hofdemel Franz	Kanzelist bei d. Ob: Just: Stelle	III
38.	Holbeinsberg Philipp Edl. von	Major von Bellegrini [Pellegrini] Infant:	I
39.	Jeschay Johann	Privatsekretär	III
40.	Justinus Johann	Stallmeister	III
41.	Kappler Joseph	Handelsmann	III
42.	Kessler Christoph Edl: von	kk: Hofsekretär	III
43.	Königsberger Joseph	Oberkom[m]is: b.d.k:k: Tobacks-Gefällen Administ.	III
44.	Kornhäusel Joh: Georg	Baumeister	III
45.	Kronauer Joh: Georg	Oeffentl: Sprachlehrer	III
46.	Kugler Franz	Haushofmeister d.Gr: Festetics	III
47.	Lepper Joseph	Fabricks Inhaber	III
48.	Lerchenthal Benedikt von	Accessist bei d.k.k. Stiftungen Hof Buchhalterei	III
49.	Ligthovler Thomas	Fabrikant	III

66

50.	Lindemayer Johann	ohne Bedienstung	III
51.	Linhardt Franz	Zuckerbäcker des Br: Leopold Kollowrath	III
52.	Mager Karl	Privat Gelehrter	III
53.	Matolay Bernh: Samuel von	k: Reichshofraths Agent	III
54.	Mechetti Karl	ohne Bedienstung	II
55.	Metz Jos: von	Offizial beim niederl. Depart:	III
56.	Mozart Wolfgang	k:k: Kapell Meister	III
57.	Münsterfeld Georg Brachtrupp von	Kanzelist bei d. Staatsraths Kanzlei	III
58.	Nemeth Joh: Samuel	der Arzneikunde Kandidat	III
59.	Niering v. Lövenfels Ant:	Konzepist b.d. geistl. Hofkom[m]ission	III
60.	Pfändler Georg	Apotheker	III
61.	Pflaum Andreas Ant:	Registrators Adjunkt b.d. O. Just. Stelle	III
62.	Plenner Ignatz	Registrant b.d. N.Ö. Regierung	III
63.	Prandtner Karl	Hausdirektor des Br: Leop: Palffy	III
64.	Reiser Leopold	Wirtschafts Rath	III
65.	Reiterer Franz	Apotheker	III
66.	Richter Philipp	Hof Trompeter	III
67.	Ried Joseph	Koch beim Br: Franz Eszterhazy	III
68.	Salat Joseph	ungar: Siebenbürg: Hof Agent	III
69.	Satsway Alexander	ungarischer Zeitungsschreiber	I
70.	Scheibenhof von Froschmayr Christoph	Ober Lieutenant	III
71.	Schmalfus Fridrich	Commis b. F: von Lobkowitz	III
72.	Schauf Franz	der Arzneikunde Doktor	III
73.	Schwartzhuber Lorenz	Magistrats Rath in Wien	I
74.	Schwingersuch Alois von	k:k Münzwardein	III
75.	Somavilla Johann	Commis beim Br: Haintz	III
76.	Starhemberg Gr: Louis	k:k: Kämmerer	III
77.	Stark Joh: Mauritz	Ober Lieut: bei Karl Toscana	II
78.	Stromer Johann	ohne Bedienstung	I
79.	Thun Joseph Gr: von	Hauptmann bei Preiss Infant:	III
80.	Traun und Abensperg Franz Eugen Gr: von	k:k: Kämmerer	III
81.	Török Joh: Nep: von	Raitrath bei der Hof Kriegs Buchhalterei	III
82.	Trummer Johann	Konzepist b.d. Bancal Gefällen Administrazion	III
83.	Wappler Christian Fridrich	Buchhändler	III
84.	Wim[m]er v. Thurnstein Gottfrid	Bancal Administrazions Dokumenten Verwalter	II
85.	Wurgo Andreas	der Arzneikunde Doktor	I
86.	Zaharadnitschek, Joseph	Trompeter bei der ungar: Leibwache	III
87.	Zeller Simon	Ober Chirurg im allgemeinen Krankenhaus	III

| 88. | Zinner Andreas | Kanzelist b.d. vereinten Hofstelle | I |
| 89. | Zitterbart Bartholome | Handelsmann | III |

Abwesende Brüder

1.	Balthaser Philipp Freih. von	Ober Lieut. bei Nassau Kürassier	III
2.	Beaumont Joh: Bap: von	Maltheser Ritter	III
3.	Benelle Joh: Karl	Chursächsischer Legazions Rath und Ober Forstkom[m]issär in Leipzig	III
4.	Berchtold Prosper Gr: von	toskanisch Stephans Ordens Ritter	III
5.	Bertrand Andreas	herrschaftl. Kom[m]issionär	III
6.	Bethlen Jos: Gr: von	k:k: Käm[m]erer u. Thesaäriats Rath in 7bürgen [Siebenbürgen]	III
7.	Bethlen Paul Gr: von	k:k: Käm[m]erer u: Gen: Major	III
8.	Biro Ladislaus von	K: Rath und Polizei Direktor in Herrmanstadt	III
9.	Bosset Franz Jos: von	Appel: Rath in Klagenfurth	III
10.	Bozenhard Joh: Gottfrid	Handelsmann in der Türkei	III
11.	Brann Wilhelm Freih: von	Fürstl: Oetting: Hof Rath und geh: Referendarius	III
12.	Brevilliers Jakob Fridrich	Banquier	III
13.	Callaghan Franz Freih: von	Ober Lieut: v: Schröder	III
14.	Callisch Max: Freih: von	Privat Kavalier	III
15.	Canal Peter Graf	Hauptmann in k: sardinischen Diensten, und Ritter des mil: Ord: der hh: Mauriz und Lazar	III
16.	Clouair Briant Karl Graf v.	Hauptmann bei Karl Toscana	III
17.	Colloredo-Metz Nik: Gr: von	k:k: Käm[m]erer u: Gen: Major	III
18.	Collin Anton	Hauptmann u. Lehrer in der milit: Schule zu W: Neustadt	III
19.	Danoz Joseph	Ingenieur Hauptmann	III
20.	De las Casas	k: spanischer Gesandter am k: neapolitanischen Hofe	III
21.	Derbey Karl	Ingenieur Ober Lieut:	I
22.	Dierkes Joseph	Rait Offizier b.d. Domainen Buchhalterei in Linz	III
23.	Dittmer Georg Frid: Edl: von	Faktor b.d. Bergprodukten Verschleis u. Banquier in Regensburg	III
24.	Doering Karl Gottlieb	Privat zu Danzig	I

68

25.	Du Jour Nikolaus	Probst zu Nikolsburg in Mähren	I
26.	Duras Joh: Jakob	Churpfalzbairischer Rath	III
27.	Dornfeld Anton von	Gub: Rath in Lemberg	III
28.	Elz Peter Franz von	Churtrierischer Finanz Rath	III
29.	Eppstein u.E:v. Ankersberg Wenzel	Gub: Sekretär in Innsbruck	III
30.	Eszterhazy Joh:Nep: Gr: von	k:k: Kämmerer und Gub: Rath zu Herrmanstadt	III
31	Fodor Joseph von	Sekretär bei d. Stadthalt: in Ofen	III
32.	Freyra d'Entrada Gomez Graf	portugiesicher Offizier und Com[m]andeur des Ordens dt Cristo	III
33.	Gammera Lud: Freih: von	k:k: Vize Konsul	III
34.	Giulay Alexius	k: Provinzial Kommissär in 7bürgen	III
35.	Giuliani Anton von	bereist die europäischen Meerhäfen auf Befehl und Kösten S: M: des Kaisers	III
36.	Gummer Franz von	Banquier in Botzen	III
37.	Günther Joh: Valentin	Hof Kriegs Sekretär bei dem Gen: Comando in 7bürgen	III
38.	Hanotte Joh: Lambert von	Kanonik[us] und Prälat zu Huy in Lüttich	III
39.	Harsch Almedingen Ludw: Gr: von	k:k: Kämmerer u: Ritter d. Steph: Ordens	III
40.	Haupt Philipp von	k:k: Rath zu Mainz	III
41.	Heister Philipp Gr: von	k:k: Käm[m]erer u. Obrist Lieut: b. Gem[m]ingen	I
42.	Herbert Franz Freih: von	Bleifabrikant in Tirol	III
43.	Hohenzollern Siegmaringen Ant: regir: Fürst zu	Reichs Erbkäm[m]erer und schwäbischer Kreis Obrister	III
44.	Hopf Phillip Heinrich	Privat Gelehrter	III
45.	Horwath Johann	Apotheker in Presburg	II
46.	Hutten Freih: von	k:k: Käm[m]erer und mil: M: Theresia Ord: Ritter und Gen: Major	III
47.	Jäger Mathias	Pfarrer zu Horn	III
48.	Kapaun Wenzel Freih: von	Rittmeister bei Harrach Kürassir	III
49.	Keller Adolph	Gren: Lieut: von Kaunitz Inf:	III
50.	Keller Gottfrid von	Registrant bei d. Landtafel in Ofen	II
51.	Kempis Max: von	Churköllnischer Käm[m]erer	II
52.	K[h]evenhuller Franz Gr: von	Lieut: bei Ligne Inf:	II
53.	Knesevics Vinzenz Freih: v:	Major bei Vukapovics Frei Korps	I
54.	Kolbani Paul	d. Arzneikunde Dok: in Presburg	I
55.	Kollonics Joseph Graf von	k:k: Käm[m]erer u: Gen: Major	III

56.	Kollowrat-Novoradsky Franz Anton Graf	k:k: wirk: geh: Rath	III
57.	Kopola de Solna Ludwig	dänischer Obrist Lieut:	III
58.	Kreyssern Johann von	Hauptmann bei Migazzi Inf:	III
59.	Kuzmics Johann von	Rathsherr zu Debreczin in Ungarn	III
60.	Lang Friedrich Wenzel	fürstl: Leiningensch: Reg: Rath	III
61	Laurenzin d'Ormond Ferd: Gr:	Lieutenant bei E:H: Franz Kaval:	III
62.	Lehrbach Ludw: Gr: von	k:k: wirk: geh: Rath und k: Kommissär bei der Reichsversammlung zu Regensburg	III
63.	Liebhardt Friedrich	Pfarrer zu Drosendorf	I
64.	Liedemann Johann	Negoziant	III
65.	Liser Joseph	Kom[m]erzial Konzepist in Triest	III
66.	Lusi Anton Spiridion Graf	preußischer Gesandter am Gros Britt: Hofe	I
67.	Maitheni Franz von	Privat Edelmann in Ungarn	II
68.	De la Marino Franz von	Gren: Hauptman[n] b. Kaiser Inf.	III
69.	Martens Johann	der Arzneikunde Dok: in Hamburg	III
70.	Merzö de Szenye Joseph	vormals Actuarius b.d. Gub: in Fiume	III
71.	Mohrenheim Jos: Freih: von	Russisch k: Hofrath, Wund u. Augen Arzt bei S:k:H: dem Großfürsten von Russland	III
72.	Montecucoli Franz Gr: von	Privatkavalier	III
73.	Montecucoli Raimund Marchese	k:k: Kämmerer und Oberster in modenesischen Diensten	II
74.	Moritsch Nikolaus	der Arzneikunde Dok: in Bozen	II
75.	Okatsch Johann	Polizei Direktor in Brünn	III
76.	Palffy Karl Graf von	Rittmeister von Erdödy	III
77.	Passy Joseph	Konzepist b.d. Domainen Güt: Administrazion in Grätz	III
78.	Pauer Johann Wolfgang	d. Rechten Doktor in Grätz	III
79.	Petersen Karl Ludwig	Sindikus zu Speyer	III
80.	Petersen Johann	vormals Sachsen Gothaischer Gesandtschafts Sekretär am k:k: Hofe	III
81.	Petran Franz	Weltpriester in Böhmen	III
82.	Pinhag Veremund	Domprediger in Laibach	III
83.	Pinterics Michael	Wirtschafts Rath des Hw: Br: Karl Palffy	III
84.	Plank Franz	Wund Artzt in Presburg	III
85.	Pronay von Toth-Pronay Ladisl: Freih: von	k:k: wirkl: geh: Rath, Ob: Gespann in Turoczer Komitat, und k: Kom[m]issär im Neusolner District	III
86.	Pronay Alexander Freih:	ohne Bedienstung	III
87.	Raday Gideon Freih: von	k: ungar Rath u. Beisitzer der Kural Tafel in Ofen	III
88.	Rheday Ludwig von	Lieutenant b. Wurmser	III

89.	Riedl Thomas Gottlieb	Gouverneur des jungen Gr: Teleky an d. Universität in Göttingen	III
90.	Salm u: Reifferscheid Karl alter Graf zu	k:k: Käm[m]erer u: Gub: Rath in Brünn	II
91.	Schlieben Jos: Freih: von	Major von Schröder Inf.	III
92.	Schnetter Frid: Ernst	Gräfl: Pappenheim: Kanzlei Direktor	III
93.	Schwediauer Franz	d. Arzneikunde Dok: in London	III
94.	Sinsteden Michael Franz	k:k: Legazionssekretär in Malta	III
95.	Spaun Felix von	k:k: Dolmetsch b.d. Armee	III
96.	Spitznagel Ferdinand	d. Arzneikunde Dok: in Ungarn	III
97.	Stambach Franz Anton Gr: von	k.k. wirkl: geh: Rath, Käm[m]erer und Vize Präsidend b.d. k: böhm Appel: Gericht in Prag	III
98.	Starhemberg Philipp Gr: von	Oberstwachtmeister	III
99.	Stein Karl Leop: Gr: von	k:k: Kämmerer, G:B:M:L: Innhaber eines Regiments Infanterie, und Komandant zu Mayland	III
100.	Sulzer Heinrich	Privat Gelehrter	III
101.	Szapari Joh: Graf von	k: Stadthalterei Rath in Ofen	III
102.	Sauer Wenzel Graf	k:k: Kämmerer, und Land Graf in Tirol	III
103.	Teleky Samuel Graf von	Rittmeister bei Nassau Küras:	III
104.	Thürheim Franz Jos: Gr: von	Ritter d. teutschen Ord: k:k: Käm[m]erer u: Gen: Major	III
105.	Vavassor Franz Edl: von	Rittmeister b. Nassau Küras:	III
106.	Vay de Vaja Nikolaus	Hauptman[n] b. Ingenieur Korps	III
107.	Vukassevics Philipp Freih: von	Ritter des Theresien Ordens u: Obrist Lieut:	III
108.	Welsberg Philipp Gr: von	k:k: geh: Rath	III
109.	Wieser Kaspar	Baumaterialien Unternehmer b.d. k:k: Portifikazionen in Böhmen	III
110.	Wilczek Joh: Jos: Graf v:	k:k: wirkl: geh: Rath, Käm[m]erer und bevollmächtigter Minister bei dem Gouvernement der Österr. Lombardei	III
111.	Wolf Joh: Nep: von	Domherr in Regensburg	III

Dienende Brüder

1.	Eckmayer Ferdinand	Kammerdiener b. Gr: Herberstein	II
2.	Goloi Simon	Bedienter b. Br: Walter	I
3.	Greli Johann	Bedienter b. Br: Sardagna	II
4.	Hiemer Joseph	Zimmerwärter der □	III
5.	Jüngling Johann	Kaffeesieder in d. Leop: Stadt	II

6.	Kessler Joseph	Kam[m]erdiener des Br: Stockham[m]ern	III
7.	Kraftmayer Joseph	Mahler	I
8.	Molitor Georg	k:k: Briefträger	III
9.	Pittlick Franz	Bedienter des Br: Calisch	I
10.	Polus Joh: Jakob	Musäums u: Bibliothek Diener	III
11.	Schwartzenbrunner Anton	Bedienter d. Br: Joh: Eszterhazy	III
12.	Sipos Joseph	Hussar d. Br: Joh: Eszterhazy	III

Hinzugekommen

Joseph Stapf   Mathematicus
Karl Julius von Lebmacher   Med: Doktor

Ausgetretten

von den anwesenden Brüdern N:° 4. und 31.